DECONSTRUCTION/
CONSTRUCTION
THE CHEONGGYECHEON RESTORATION PROJECT IN SEOUL

DECONSTRUCTION/ CONSTRUCTION
THE CHEONGGYECHEON RESTORATION PROJECT IN SEOUL

The Tenth Veronica Rudge Green Prize in Urban Design

Edited by Joan Busquets

HARVARD UNIVERSITY GRADUATE SCHOOL of DESIGN

ISBN 978-1-934510-31-5

Book design by Jared James May, series design by Kim Shkapich
Cover: Diagram by Joan Busquets
Inside front cover: Image by Sae-Hyun Kim
Printed and bound by Puritan Press

The Harvard University Graduate School of Design is a leading center for education, information, and technical expertise on the built environment. Its departments of Architecture, Landscape Architecture, and Urban Planning and Design offer masters and doctoral degree programs and provide the foundation for its Advanced Studies and Executive Education programs.

PREFACE
Mohsen Mostafavi

The Veronica Rudge Green Prize's recognition of the project for the recovery of the Cheong-gyecheon River is a marker of historic and geographic significance in the formation of the city of Seoul. The Cheonggyecheon Restoration Project, an undertaking of great scope and commensurate positive impact, is a worthy recipient on this milestone tenth occasion of the awarding of the prize.

This also happens to be the year during which the Graduate School of Design is celebrating the 50th Anniversary of its Urban Design Program. The fortuitous combination of these two events is a testimony to the School's ongoing commitment to the value of improving the quality of public space across the globe.

For it is the interaction of the architecture of the city with the diversity of its symbolic, infrastructural, and commercial networks that creates the settings for the unfolding of the lives of citizens. In this way, the physical fabric of a city provides an enabling social and political framework for everyday life. The restoration of the Cheonggyecheon River not only establishes this framework but also aims to create an ecological habitat in the midst of a major metropolis. It is the value of the project simultaneously as an infrastructural, cultural, sustainable, and pleasurable urban intervention that makes it so deserving of the Green Prize.

Rarely do government agencies take such bold actions and make plans for large-scale territorial projects that transcend the mere pragmatic necessities of the city. In this case, however, the approach is highly consistent with a renaissance of interest in all design-related fields. This might also help account for the fact that the awarding of the Veronica Rudge Green Prize is the second time in the past twelve months that the Graduate School of Design has exhibited an architectural project from Korea. During the Fall of the 2009–2010 academic year, a major exhibition as part of the series New Trajectories featured contemporary architecture, landscape architecture, and urban projects from that country.

Even though there is increasing interest in environmental issues worldwide, the focus of this attention remains primarily at the scale of individual buildings. I am grateful for the generous financial support of the von Clemm family and to the Michael and Louisa von Clemm Foundation for making it possible for the GSD to be among the few institutions to recognize and promote design excellence and sustainability at the urban scale. Many thanks are also due to my colleague Joan Busquets and the award jury, whose rigorous evaluation of many nominations resulted in the selection of this remarkable project.

ACKNOWLEDGMENTS
Joan Busquets

I take great pleasure in expressing my sincere appreciation to the many people and organizations that have made this publication possible. I would like to thank the Seoul Metropolitan Government and the Mayor's Office for supplying materials documenting the Cheonggyecheon Restoration Project. Klee Yong-Jae Yang, Jongho Shin, Min Ryung Seo, and their teams deserve great thanks for their help during the process of gathering material for this book and the related GSD exhibition. I would like to express my gratitude to Heung-Sun Kim, Tae-Gyu Koh, and Kie-Wook Kwon of Cheonggyecheon Management Team for the descriptive material they provided for the publication, and to Chang-Bok Yim and Kiho Kim for their special insights into the project.

For their invaluable contributions, thanks go to the members of the tenth Green Prize Jury: Eve Blau, Adjunct Professor in Architectural History; Chris Reed, Adjunct Associate Professor of Landscape Architecture; and Marion Weiss, Graham Professor of Architecture at the University of Pennsylvania and, with Michael Manfredi, recipient of the 2007 Veronica Rudge Green Prize in Urban Design. The task of selecting the project from almost 100 interesting experiences across the globe was a challenging one.

I would like to thank Peter Rowe, the Raymond Garbe Professor of Architecture and Urban Design and University Distinguished Service Professor. He and his team, especially Kristen Hunter, Sanghoon Jung, Saehoon Kim, and Pilsoo Ming, deserve our special thanks for the material they provided from their own research that informed both book and exhibition.

I would also like to express my deepest gratitude to Dan Borelli, Shannon Stecher, and David Stuart of the GSD Exhibitions Department, and warmest thanks as well to the participating GSD students and recent graduates from various programs: Sae-Hyun Kim, Donghwan Moon, Megan Panzano, Clara Lee, and Erik Prince.

My thanks also go to Melissa Vaughn for her help in producing this book and to Jared May for his design work, within a series design by Kim Shkapich. Finally, I would like to thank Ian Klein for his untiring work as research assistant to the jury, preparing materials for the selection process and helping to make this book possible.

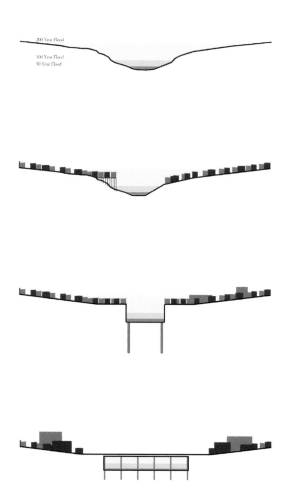

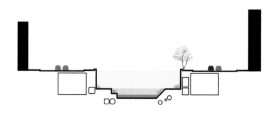

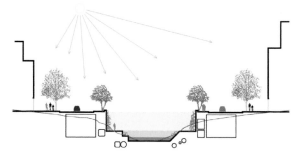

Evolution of the valley section from natural to urban condition, 1700-2015.

THE CHEONGGYECHEON RESTORATION PROJECT:
THE DECONSTRUCTION AND CONSTRUCTION OF A MAJOR METROPOLITAN SPACE IN SEOUL

Joan Busquets

Seoul, a fascinating global city with a furious pace of urban growth, has recently recovered one of its seminal central spaces by transforming an elevated highway with heavy traffic flows at the heart of the city into a multipurpose public space of an unprecedented size, in record time. The restoration of this space showcases the original stream on the banks of which the city was founded.

The decision to award the project the Veronica Rudge Green Prize in Urban Design and the deliberations of the jury raise a number of provocative questions:

1. Does the Cheonggyecheon Restoration Project represent a new phase in the progressive urbanization of the stream or a new concept of the use of central space?

2. Is the project a prelude to a new scale for urban transformations in the twenty-first century?

3. Is it possible to see the Cheonggyecheon Restoration Project, in both form and content, as a paradigm for new public spaces at the scale of the large global city?

Cheonggyecheon: A Vital Watercourse for Seoul

Since antiquity, humankind's relationship with rivers has been interpreted in many ways, as a powerful emotional and poetic association. Human settlements have reflected this relation, seeing the river as a basic infrastructure around which many towns and cities have been structured. As a concept, this varies greatly depending on whether the water body is a stream, usually with lower water levels, or a larger, more continuous river that may present a barrier yet also offer greater potential for transport and the harnessing of energy, creating ideal places to set up production activities.

Cheonggyecheon belongs to the first group. Its water level varies considerably, depending on rainfall, making the definition of its limits somewhat problematic. Various cultures have coined special names for this widely variable condition, such as the Spanish *barranco* or *arroyo*, and the Italian *fiumara*, which expresses the idea that this watercourse "is a river but can become a sea," depending on the amount of rain. This is the case of Cheonggyecheon, which perhaps explains why the city previously developed secondary settlements and complementary activities rather than siting formal activities beside the stream, considering the land unsafe. Nonetheless, the stream is a point of reference in historical images of Seoul.

The Long Journey from Stream to Waterside Promenade

Cheonggyecheon was probably a decisive factor in choosing the site of the city, a selection informed by principles of geomancy or feng shui in Korea. Four hills of around 300 meters in height surround the foundational space and still frame what is a seminal center for the metropolis.

The city's foundational relation with its geography seems to respond to a universal concept, the prototypical "valley section" that Patrick Geddes posited a century ago. He reminds us how civilization evolves in its valley position according to the dominant activities of each age, from nomadism to fishing, to farming and then to urban life; its situation in the valley evolves with the way people settle and live. The stream presents water as a way for the settlement to grow, leading to the development of districts along its tributaries. Later, growth calls for more stable means of provisioning, and the stream becomes important for complementary activities such as washing, drainage, etc. In addition, flood-prevention measures tend to increasingly separate the stream from the activities carried out in its immediate surroundings.

In the second half of the last century, infrastructures related to mobility began to acquire importance, and the concept of hierarchy became essential to their organization. This led to broader, straighter layouts to increase their capacity. The new streets were therefore wider, and extensions

Early settlement patterns along the river were primarily densely packed informal houses.

were introduced into existing urban fabric at the cost of major demolition work. Taller buildings with new functional programs sprang up, often asphyxiating the traditional city. Given this trend, it is no wonder that some cities started to use their riverside spaces to accommodate major road infrastructures. This was the case of Seoul and Cheonggyecheon, which was paved over. The process culminated in the construction between 1956 and 1970 of an elevated highway to siphon off traffic to the viaduct from city approach roads. (It is also the case of São Paulo and its river Tietê, the section of which is, for the most part, doubled by its overpass.) Similarly, in more recent decades Seoul situated its major road infrastructures along the large Hangang river, again cutting off natural access to the waterfront.

In this way, cities erase the important traces of their natural geography and begin a process of superposition of different specialities (water, sewerage, and private and segregated transport) that have little potential for introducing a new dialogue with the city and surrounding activities. The greatest merits of the Cheonggyecheon project have been: 1) the understanding of deconstruction as a constructive process, but also as a logic of intervention, and 2) the integrated implantation of specialized systems (sewerage, services, flood protection, water table, different circulation flows, etc.), seen from the viewpoint of the urban project, which allows them to coexist but also makes them an active, essential part of the city and the urban fabric. Some specific characteristics of the project are addressed below.

Piers are erected to support the road covering the river in 1965.

The Multiple Scales of Seoul Metropolitan City

At this point, it is interesting to set the city's urbanistic evolution in the context of the transformation of infrastructure. Although there are prehistoric vestiges dating back more than 5,000 years, Seoul is a city with a history of about six centuries, beginning when it was named capital in 1394 by the Joseon Dynasty. It was restored to its role as capital in 1949 after the period of Japanese domination (1910–1945), though the Korean War, lasting until 1949, resulted in the destruction of much of the preexisting city. Its explosive growth began in 1960, when it had 2.5 million inhabitants, reaching 10 million by 1990.

The foundational city was built with a grid layout, like Xi'An in China—the point of reference for the foundation of many Asian cities; Kyoto also seems to follow this pattern. Digital technologies have accustomed us to the idea that a synthetic reading of big cities—recently considered so complex and broad as to make a comprehensive view impossible—is not only feasible but actually very common. Readings presented by Google maps and Bing are leading naturally to new cross-scale interpretations and are accessible to the majority of the global population. They have reintroduced the formal conditions of the city, including large cities such as Seoul, making them easy to grasp. This new means of visualization has huge potential and seems

River embankments are formed and reinforced prior to covering the river.

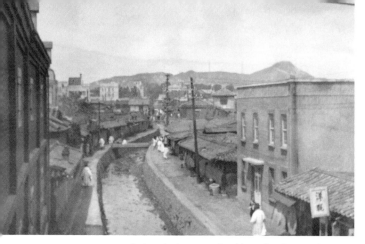

Early embankment works mitigate flood impacts but disconnected the river from the city.

Prior to its covering, the river was densely lined with informal housing on stilts.

likely to have positive repercussions, finally dispersing cloud of ignorance hovering over big cities as a result of inability of prior technologies to read and interpret them

We cannot ignore the need to investigate other new ways reading the metropolis that go beyond the simple functio diagrams that we are used to seeing in guidebooks. A such as Seoul can be explained by its monuments, town w and bridges, and even simple buildings like its *hanoks*, acco panied by the historical narrative of certain key dates. understand the impact of Cheonggyecheon on the grea metropolis, however, it is useful to introduce a broader re ing based on the urban morphologies that make up this re ity and provide some pointers as to the processes of mo fication and transformation. A morphological classificat serves to explain: 1) the process of physical construct of the city and its parts, including constituent elements a formal contents such as plot size, scope of the venture, ty of building, dominant uses, etc., and 2) the various requir ments in terms of investment and management capacities the agents involved in the construction of the city.

This observation is perhaps relevant to a specific di plinary reading for Seoul and helps to understand the for of transformation that can be promoted in the mid-ter Only a more precise interpretation will lead to an ove understanding of interventions in infrastructure and put space in relation to processes in the urban fabric, showing potential for improvement. They are necessary to the evo tion of Seoul if it is to avoid the conclusion that cities wit fast pace of construction are fated to continue their pro esses of eradication and replacement of preceding pha as the only way to modernize or update their residen and urban fabrics. The Cheonggyecheon project, convers seems to suggest scenarios in which the superposition major interventions in content and program combines w operations of rehabilitation of the existing fabric.

Morphological analyses carried out to gauge the impact of the Cheonggyecheon project show that, since its great population explosion began in 1960, the city has extended its bounds but also tripled its residential density, with an increase from 60 to 170 inhabitants per hectare. At the same time, Seoul is also consolidating a series of highly determinant morphologies, such as:

- Low-rise houses that follow the street layout and occupy a large surface area, with small interstitial spaces between houses.

- Small buildings of collective housing organized for multifamily use.

- Squatter-type self-construction systems based on rural patterns, producing the so-called moon cities on steep hillsides.

- *Tanji*, which are modern residential complexes defined by systems of detached blocks (housing estates). They now represent half of the dwellings in Seoul and are associated with an image of modernization of the country. It is important to note that *tanji* are not social housing; they are middle-class homes, and it is considered a privilege to live in them. Most of them are condominiums, stabilizing the population. The space in which they are set is generally collective, belonging to the complex, with an elected trustee and a gate attendant.

Though at first glance they may seem like European housing estates, such as the central European *Siedlungen*, other factors distinguish them as having their roots in the tradition of residential complexes such as the company town, associated with industries or rural settlements. These references suggest something more along the lines of Clarence Perry's neighborhood unit in the United States in the 1920s than the European *Siedlungen*. In the

This residential and retail megastructure by Kim Soo Geun Sewoon is one of several modernist-influenced urban pieces along the river.

To increase mobility to the downtown core, an elevated expressway was erected above the street covering the Cheonggyecheon.

development of the *tanji*, it is important to highlight the role of the state more as a guarantor, offering fiscal support, than an actual constructor.

These complexes constitute an element of modernization of the country "without modernity." Although the influence of modern thought seems to be behind them, it lies more in the types and the general morphology than in a cultural or stylistic attitude. The modernity of Le Corbusier was introduced by some of his Korean disciples, particularly Kim Chungop, who in 1957 manifested the modern language in Konguk University Library, and in 1970 in the building for Kukche insurance company. German influence was apparent in the construction of Chongam residential complex, a pioneering housing initiative.

Kim Soo Geun's Sewoon Project of 1956 was an outstanding attempt to produce an interesting mixed residential unit in the form of a megastructure perpendicular to Cheonggyecheon, following the principles of Team X and the Metabolist movement in Japan. It is a complex comprising four blocks that cross the streets with a built system of various levels, including shops on the lower floors, with a raised walkway on the fifth floor, above which the main use is residential. The restoration of Cheonggyecheon will help to rehabilitate this singular element, currently in a state of abandonment that could be associated with the deterioration caused by the heavy infrastructure on the site. The current-day metropolis is, then, like a collage of morphologies and infrastructures undergoing a far-reaching transformation. This involves the gradual creation of a grid of traffic avenues of increasing width to accommodate greater traffic flows.

The country's functional and economic modernization came in the 1980s with the 1986 Asian Games; the 1988 Olympic Games represented a qualitative leap that led to further economic and political evolution. Shortly afterward, the 2002 World Cup ushered in other conditions and models for the contemporary city that are still largely operative. This process was accompanied by the development and expansion of large companies that were consolidated and grew as a result of the construction of these major infrastructures.

Seoul can be said to be embarking on a phase of prioritizing projects that aspire to spatial singularity, in keeping with the scale of other metropolises it has in its sights. It is interesting to highlight efforts to define model districts, such as Creative City and the promotion of Seoul as World Design Capital for late 2010; although this initiative came from within the city, it represents its concern with the field of creativity. Also worthy of mention is the current project for Dongdaemun Design Plaza and Park by Zaha Hadid, to replace a former stadium with scant practical application and create a small centrality. The discovery of the ruins of the old town wall and the east gateway during groundbreaking gives the project a new value that integrates the old structure of the city with the modernity that imbues its activities.

Designing at the Large Scale

The Cheonggyecheon Restoration Project aims to represent a new phase in the urbanization of the original watercourse in the context of the huge potential of present-day metropolitan reality. The project represents a general hypothesis of the role of this complex of infrastructures in the mid-term and seeks to integrate this stretch of the stream into the hydraulic system as a whole.

Modern infrastructures have been based primarily on the section, with recourse to guidelines that produced projects that were efficient in time and competitive in cost. These were the principles used to design previous phases in the development of Cheonggyecheon. The next step is to redesign the stream as an urban space that is capable of addressing hydraulic issues and infrastructure of all kinds, as well as constructing a fragment of the city's system of natural spaces.

To this end, the project seems to adopt the definition of an open boulevard running between the city blocks that border it. The avenue, of an average width of 50 meters (varying between 40 and 80 meters), defines a continuous plan of connection with the rest of the urban space and accommodates a depressed central system comprising the streambed and its terraces. It incorporates three levels separated by between 2 and 6 meters, with a well-defined general form, interconnected by ramps and bridges. The top level (the boulevard in the city) will still require a complementary process of redesign as the transformation of the stream's banks develops.

The first project decision would seem to be the geometry of this variable section and the way in which the various surfaces of the section are to be addressed. The urban design project calls for the right proportion between the levels of the project and its judicious insertion into the urban fabric of the central city. The project skillfully addresses the difference between the invisible infrastructures subject to an underground logic and the visible infrastructures that have to be reconciled with the various everyday uses required by a central space of this nature.

The demolition of the elevated highway and the restoration of the stream formed the core of the city's cultural and urbanistic debate. It was during the 2002 campaign of the future mayor, Myung-bak Lee (who has since become the country's president), and his team that the foundations were laid for the project to be carried out in a period of twenty-seven months, including the careful deconstruction of the viaduct (which alone took ten months), the execution of the underground infrastructure, and the construction of the public space.

The Cheonggyecheon Restoration Project was clear in its brief and divided into three different sectors (carried out by three firms: Daelim, Samsung, and Hyundai), following the turnkey model. It was coordinated by the city's municipal team. The project was entrusted with integrating different logics (rainwater, sewerage, storm water, connections across streets, etc.), creating a new paradigm. In this, it is comparable to Burnham and Bennett's Wacker Drive in Chicago, designed in 1926. This mile-long linear space along the river established a system of multiple levels to efficiently organize various uses and functions in the downtown of this dynamic city and provide a new model for future projects.

Another interesting reference is the reurbanization of the Danube Canal in Vienna to make it navigable, by Otto Wagner and his team (1894–1908). This important hydraulic project introduced a system of wharfs and a high-profile boulevard into the cityscape. Wagner acted as artistic advisor to the Commission for the Regulation of the Danube. Within the macro urban design project, he was responsible for the Nussdorf sluice gate and Kaiserbad Dam, and the broad new boulevard.

A New Paradigm for Reinterpreting Large-Scale Global Cities?

Like Vienna, Seoul illustrates the ability of urban design projects to come up with ingenious, lasting solutions that generate a quality, sustainable city. Such projects often do not have a single designer and, in most cases, they require exemplary political support and public negotiation. They also call for great structural efficiency and an effective management process, without which they can easily become exhausting and controversial. We might say that the very concept of urban design implicitly involves certain principles of execution without which the broader view is impossible.

The broad positive impact of the Cheonggyecheon urban design project figured strongly in the discussions of the jury of the Veronica Rudge Green Prize. City design cannot be regarded merely as the product of an inspired designer or a skillful politician, though the selfless task of city formalization is vital to good city design: the complexity of urban processes and decision-making and the

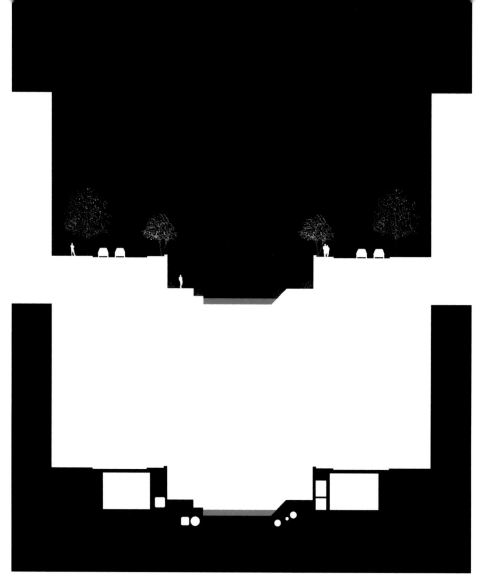

The intervention reorganizes both visible and invisible systems to transform the city.

power of single-minded forces interested only in achieving their own ends make city construction a difficult undertaking. In the case of Cheonggyecheon, the presence and constant support of Mayor Lee, the work of the urban design group, the coordination of the metropolitan government, and the contributions of the specialists and engineers from various firms resulted in a brilliant and effective team, as the results show.

In this process, the urban design project becomes the common ground on which differing competencies and specialities come together. The project establishes formal logics and systems of synergy between disciplines and between specialized sectors. This strategy of bringing together technical and artistic disciplines, doers and thinkers, creates a new paradigm that addresses questions of urban form and townscape and the integration of various flows, and offers a new interpretation of this fragment of the city that goes beyond its spatial bounds.

The large scale of the project suggests a different urbanistic direction for the transformation of Seoul and its metropolitan system: this could be a new relation between landscape and geography, or a new way of dissolving the landscape into the existing city. Among other things, the project strengthens the right bank of the river Hangang between Gangbuk and Gangnam, the site of most modern developments beginning with Yeouido Island and the Olympic developments of 1988.

The Cheonggyecheon project could help to construct a new paradigm for public space within the Korean tradition, in which formal civic space traditionally plays a minor part. The recent example of Seoul Plaza in front of City Hall (2002) stands out as the transformation of a road intersection into a civic space with an important role in the city's collective life. Cheonggyecheon represents a commitment to a new kind of public space that shares the values posited by Hannah Arendt (space for public action), Jürgen Habermas (civic space for public opinion), and Henri Lefebvre (space of centrality).

The Cheonggyecheon project also tables the question as to whether public space should be seen as empty or full. There is a tradition that persists in considering urban space as empty, though not of meaning, inspired by Far Eastern thinking. Maurice Merleau-Ponty wrote that the appearance of the world would be altered if we were to see the intervals between things—for example, the spaces between the trees in the boulevard—as objects in themselves. The top surface of the project, represented by the boulevard, allows for the addition of further values to those established at the lower levels. The addition of another layer introduces the possibility of understanding that the empty space is filled, seeking to integrate the visible and the invisible into the central public space. In short, Cheonggyecheon is a thought-provoking project at the scale of Greater Seoul, notable for its capacity to create new urban spaces in which centrality is always possible, allowing or creating the potential for the unforeseen and the unforeseeable.

Bibliography

Gelézeau, Valérie. *Séoul, ville géante, cités radieuses.* Paris: CNRS éditions, 2003.

Kwak, Heui-Jeong. *A Turning Point in Korea's Urban Modernization: The Case of the Sewoon Sangga Development.* Cambridge: 2002.

Mantziaras, Panos. *Rudolf Schwarz et la dissolution des villes. La ville Paysage.* Geneva: Metis Presses, 2008.

Queysanne, Bruno. *Philosophie et/de l'architecture.* Grenoble: Cahiers de pensée et d'histoire de l'architecture, no. 4, 1985.

Seoul Metropolitan Government. *Urban Planning of Seoul.* Seoul: 2010.

Wagner, Otto. *Architecture moderne et autres écrits.* Brussels: Pierre Mardaga, 1984.

Welter, Volker M. *Biopolis: Patrick Geddes and the City of Life.* Cambridge, MA: MIT Press, 2002.

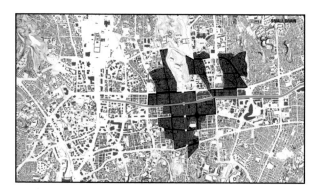

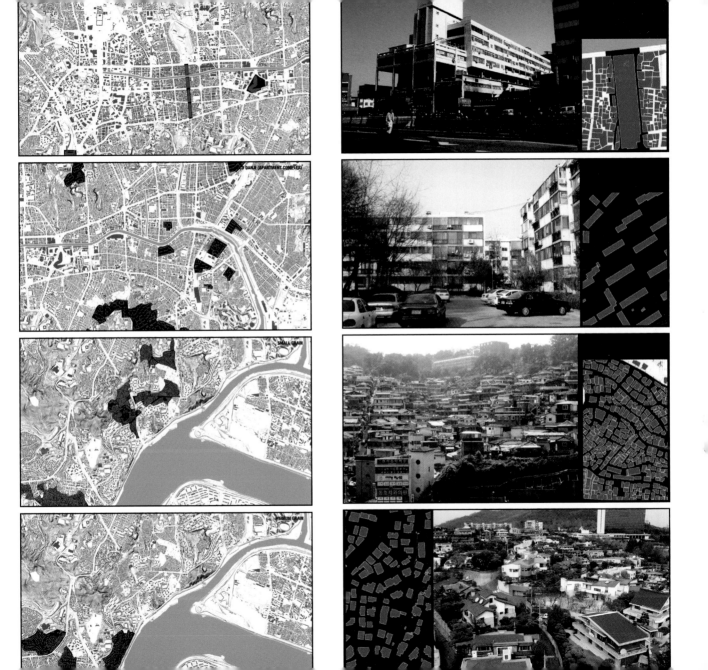

Seoul as a city has always existed—over time in increasingly greater density—in the space between the Han River and its tributaries and the surrounding mountains. The Cheonggyecheon is at the center of this dialogue; along its path, the Cheongyecheon acts as a spine for a diverse host of highly determinant urban morphologies.

RECALIBRATING THE URBAN

Eve Blau

The Cheonggyecheon River Restoration Project is an extraordinary feat of engineering and farsighted planning, and an act of political will that has transformed the center of Seoul. A 3-mile-long stream of running water, alive with plants, fish, birds, and urban citizens at leisure, now flows through the dense urban fabric of the downtown. In the laconic terms of planning discourse, the Cheonggyecheon Restoration Project replaced a mobility asset (the multilevel highway that had covered the river since the early 1960s) and safety hazard with an urban amenity. The surgical precision with which the massive elevated concrete roadbeds and ramps were removed—in record time and with minimal noise, dust, and other pollutants—is exemplary in itself. So too, is the careful construction of the pedestrian pathways, vertical channel walls, new sewage system, and ecologically sophisticated and informed planting of the riverbanks.

But the project is far more extensive than the linear park. Environmentally, the restored waterway and plantings have not only changed the ecology along its banks but have affected the climatic conditions within a certain radius of the stream, cutting air pollution and even lowering the ambient temperature by as much as 5 degrees in the summer months. Economically, the Cheonggyecheon is said to have stimulated business activity in the surrounding area and, for the first time in Seoul's modern history, has effectively linked the economically and cultural advantaged south side of the city to the less advantaged northern sections, and generated a new cultural space and tourist attraction at their core. Rather than exacerbating traffic congestion in the center (with the removal of the much-trafficked highways), the project actually reduced pressure on the central business district by increasing the transportation capacity of buses and subways, and redirecting motor traffic. Cheonggyecheon is an urban intervention with far-reaching significance for the city as a whole.

But what about the issue of urban design? What lessons regarding the design of urban space and fabric in the contemporary city can we learn from the Cheonggyecheon Restoration Project? The first, I would suggest, is the issue of scale, or more precisely, the instrumentality of design at the middle scale—between architecture and planning—and the organizational capacity of urban design to project beyond the parameters of the physical intervention. The Cheonggyecheon Restoration Project is a circumscribed intervention. While it daylights the river and generates a linear park along its length, it does not significantly expand its girth. Yet in terms of instrumentality, it projects far beyond the spatial and temporal boundaries of its site. Spatially, it forges a much-needed connection between parts of the city that had been divided by cultural amenity and disparate levels of economic development. It does so at the scale of the existing fabric, carefully knitting together new and old bridges, pedestrian pathways and new sidewalks, and existing urban passageways and thoroughfares that penetrate deep into the center of the flanking urban districts. In doing so, it restores not only the biological ecology of the original river but its social ecology as well, generating new spaces for everyday use (people from the surrounding shops and businesses take their lunches to the park, go for midday walks, and enjoy evening entertainment) and extending the intimate scale and spatial diversity of these ecologies deep into the larger urban ecosystem of Seoul's center.

The Cheonggyecheon projects temporally beyond the physical limits of its site as well. By restoring the east-west waterway along which the original urban settlement of Seoul occurred, it recovers the history of the central space of Seoul city. This history includes not only the river and its embankments, the long-destroyed wooden houses that had been built on stilts along its frequently flooded banks (a small number of which have been reconstructed as part of the Cheonggyecheon Museum) but also remnants of the concrete pylons that had supported the elevated highway and other pieces of industrial archeology from the 1960s. But most important are the still vital pieces of that history and fabric: the traditional single-story shops and small businesses in the machine trades that open onto and spill into the streets on either side of the Cheonggyecheon, and the massive

wholesale markets and shopping arcades—megastructures filled with thousands of tiny establishments selling every conceivable appliance, machine part, household and office furnishing, electronic device, and type of clothing—that have been the heart and soul of the market culture in the area for the last half century. Today the vital connection between the restored Cheonggyecheon river and this vibrant local culture and economy is more tangible and appears to be more self-sustaining than the new translocal culture belt, green network, and business area that the Cheonggyecheon is projected to generate across its axis. It is hoped that the new business area will not disturb this delicate ecology. Currently the process by which the Cheonggyecheon connects past and present, old and new fabric, existing and emerging spatial patterns is dialogic. Spatial and temporal layers coexist and together actualize the contemporary city as a place that is not so much formed by history as it is a place of agency where the future is shaped—where history is made.

There is another way in which the Cheonggyecheon engages the issue of scale in urban design. The multiplicity of factors involved in the design and execution of the project itself—from plant ecology to traffic and water regulation, and the design and integration of discrete urban and architectural objects including lighting fixtures, bridges, viaducts, sustaining walls, staircases, ramps, stepping stones, service structures, seating facilities, and other pieces of street furniture—comprises every scale of intervention from the individual object to the fully integrated urban infrastructural system. The design issues are complex and undermine the fixed categories—building, infrastructure, city, landscape, region—by which we have traditionally distinguished scales of design intervention. They demand design thinking at multiple scales and solutions that reconcile complexity with control. Most of all, they make it clear that traditional disciplinary divisions no longer hold in the face of the multifactorial interdependency and complexity of projects such as Cheonggyecheon.

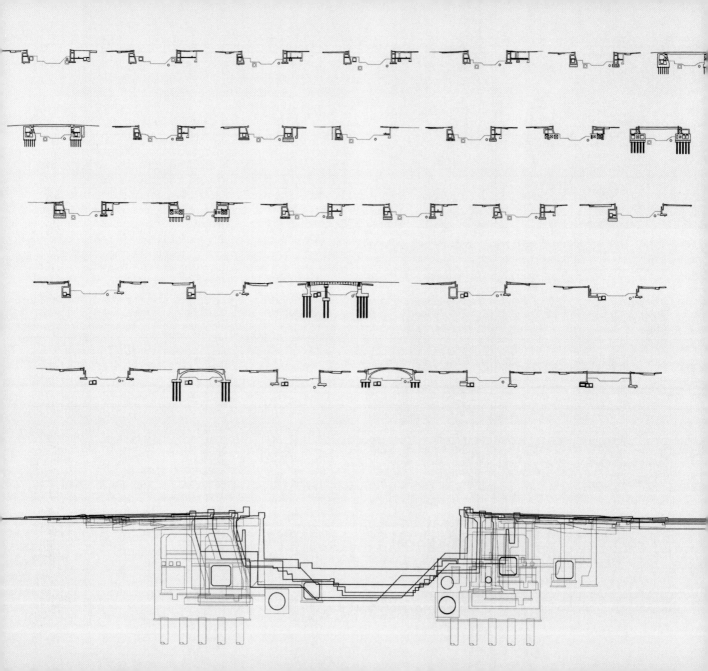

They force us to recognize that infrastructural moves have architectural implications, that design encompasses the natural as well as the built environment (both are tied to evolving technologies of communication and production), and that architecture involves formulating solutions at many scales, from the individual object to the territory. Most of all, these conditions make it clear that we need continuously to recalibrate the urban.

How can we understand the conditions of change, extreme differentiation, and hybridity that challenge current conceptual models and practices? The urban, according to Henri Lefebvre, is a condition, not a thing. It is a spatial formation in which the logic of form is associated with the dialectic of content—a condition in which form and content continuously shape and transform each other. It is, Lefebvre contends, a "concrete abstraction, associated with practice."[1] How does this idea relate to urban design?

First, it suggests that design—as a spatial practice—involves both the generation of authored form and the production of content (that is, ideas/meaning) and that the relationship between them is unstable and dynamic. Second, it helps us to understand urban design practices as not only a matter of intervening in the city but also of reading the city in a certain way—as project and projection—that is, in terms of practice and the production and transfer of particular kinds of spatial knowledge. Finally, it underscores the fact that design is inherently projective and propositional.

These ideas enable us to understand the larger techno-social and cultural significance of the Cheonggyecheon Restoration Project. The demolition of the multilevel highway and reconstruction of the ancient Cheonggyecheon river and its natural and social ecologies was in many ways the physical enactment of the enormous transition in Korean economic and social life from the period of intense urbanization and economic

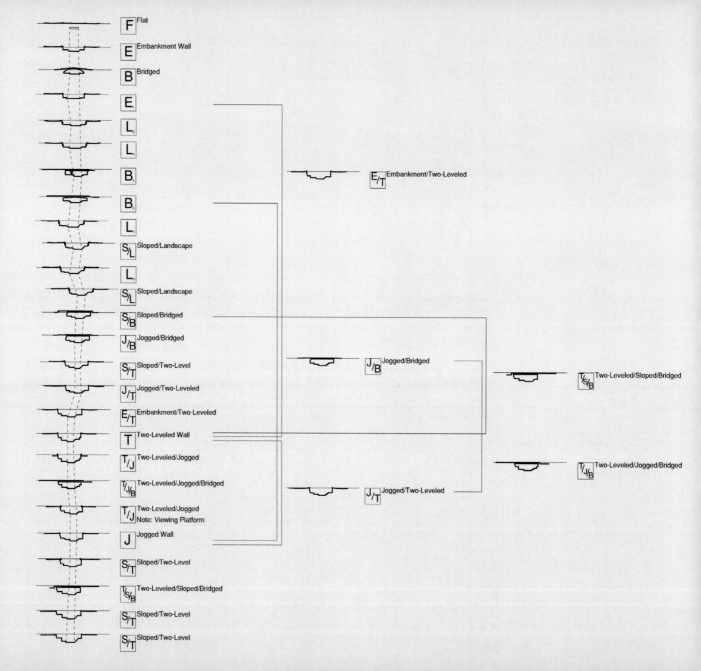

F   Flat

E   Embankment Wall

B   Bridged

E

L

L

B

B

L

S/L   Sloped/Landscape

L

S/L   Sloped/Landscape

S/B   Sloped/Bridged

J/B   Jogged/Bridged

S/T   Sloped/Two-Level

J/T   Jogged/Two-Leveled

E/T   Embankment/Two-Leveled

T   Two-Leveled Wall

T/J   Two-Leveled/Jogged

T/J/B   Two-Leveled/Jogged/Bridged

T/J   Two-Leveled/Jogged
Note: Viewing Platform

J   Jogged Wall

S/T   Sloped/Two-Level

T/S/B   Two-Leveled/Sloped/Bridged

S/T   Sloped/Two-Level

S/T   Sloped/Two-Level

E/T   Embankment/Two-Leveled

J/B   Jogged/Bridged

J/T   Jogged/Two-Leveled

T/S/B   Two-Leveled/Sloped/Bridged

T/J/B   Two-Leveled/Jogged/Bridged

development (based on export-oriented industrialization, principally ship building, automobile manufacture, consumer electronics, and construction) known as the "Miracle on the Han" in which the emphasis spatially was on the efficient circulation of goods and people through the urban territory. This was the economy that built the roadbed and elevated highway over the Cheonggyecheon River in the 1960s and 1970s.[2] Its demolition in 2003 and replacement by the Cheonggyecheon Restoration Project signaled the dominance of a new urban economic engine, one driven by network technologies and the co-evolution of media-cultural and digital communication technologies (mobile telephones, broadband, and internet) in contemporary Korean industry. Known as the "Korean Wave," this economy places new value on consumer choice and individual desire, on "lifestyle" and urban amenity.[3] Whereas Seoul was conceived in the 1960s by the then mayor as "the city is lines" (circulation: wires and roads), today its aspiration is to be the media-saturated "Ubiquitous City" (or U-City) of ambient informatics, connected locally and globally through networks and nodes.

In this context, the Cheonggyecheon Restoration Project constitutes a new kind of urban space in Seoul—a space of "typological obscurity," multiply coded as park, city square, technical infrastructure, cultural institution, wildlife habitat—for a broad range of unspecified and informal uses. It affords its visitors both company and solitude, connection and detachment, possibilities for rest and activity, objects of study and of aesthetic pleasure. But the true novelty of the Cheonggyecheon as an urban space is the fact that it combines the "rush of high-tech cyberspace and nature in one central-Seoul spot."[4] In 2007 residents and foreign tourists were invited on the official government website to "Experience Ubiquitous Seoul at Cheonggyecheon Event."[5] At Cheonggyecheon the material and the virtual, the physical,

and the digital are uniquely meshed. The "natural" landscape is technologically sustained—the water is pumped uphill from the Han, purified, and monitored by high-tech instruments and systems. Visitors can interact with the plants and wildlife, enjoy the sound, smell, and feel of the rushing water, and enhance those experiences by accessing the "Interactive Media Boards" (which provide information about Cheonggyecheon) and share their experiences and send digital postcards from the "Free Boards" located in the park. LED-equipped street lamps, that are also internet hotspots, and vending machines that sell USB keys preloaded with historical and tourist information about the stream are also part of the "Ubiquitous Service Zone" at the Cheonggyecheon river site.[6]

Cheonggyecheon, like other particularly Korean conceptions of social space—such as Bangs (reconfigurable spaces of inhabitation and/or commerce that are designed to support a multiplicity of functions[7]) and the U-City of ubiquitous information technology—is a multiply coded space shaped by an action-based design logic conceived in terms of experience rather than form. It is an environment where public and private are relational and contingent rather than absolute conditions, determined by use and actions rather than discrete volumes. Public space is generated by interaction, private space by withdrawing from company. Both can occur anywhere.

The city itself, where the connectivity of the information society intersects with the physical spaces of daily life and work, is conceived as situated at the intersection of the material and the virtual, as fundamentally mutable, continuously negotiating, adapting to, and interacting with equally dynamic and mutable social and technological environments. Its spaces are shaped by the confluence of global technologies of communication and information transfer, and local modes of inhabitation, use, and information exchange.

previous pages New public space for art.
opposite Recombinant sectional conditions.

The Cheonggyecheon river project, as a new kind of hybrid urban space that purports to merge cyberspace with nature, underscores the historical knowledge that "information processing is an age-old function of cities."[8] At the same time, however, this new kind of hybrid urban space does not erase the cognitive gap between the worlds of information and experience. Instead, it makes us continuously aware of the contradictions between those worlds and reminds us that the city itself "is our original and greatest information technology."[9]

1. Henri Lefebvre, *The Urban Revolution*, trans. Robert Bononno (Minneapolis and London: 2003), 118–119.

2. Jaz Hee-Jeong Choi and Adam Greenfield, "To Connect and Flow in Seoul: Ubiquitous Technologies, Urban Infrastructure, and Everyday Life in the Contemporary Korean City," in Marcus Foth, editor, *Urban Informatics: The Practice and Promise of the Real-Time City* (Hershey, NY: Information ScienceReference, 2009): 22–23.

3. Ibid., 23. See also Jaz Hee-Jeong Choi, "The Korean Wave of U.," in H.K. Anheier and Y.R. Isar, editors, *The Cultures of Globalization Series: The Cultural Economy* (London: Sage, 2008).

4. Korea.net, 2007.

5. Ibid.

6. www.futurizekorea.com/entry/u-cheonggyecheon-interaction-displays (January 6, 2008).

7. See Sung Hong Kim, "City of the Bang." Ninth International Architecture Exhibition, 2004 Venice Biennale. [http://www.korean-pavilion.or.k/04pavilion/e_2004_02.htm]

8. Anthony Townsend, "Foreword," in Foth, ed., *Urban Informatics*, xxiii.

9. Ibid.

The river became contaminated and unhygienic due to years of being used for citywide debris and sewage conveyance.

Initial covering of the river in the form of multimodal bridges to convey people and goods across the river.

The covered Cheonggyecheon became a heavyweight mobility infrastructure accommodating multiple speeds and forms of transport.

While remnants of the former infrastructure are preserved as artifacts, the current manifestation of the Cheonggyecheon has become a hybrid infrastructure that accommodates urban utilitarian needs, natural ecosystems, and an interactive public space network.

THE ECOLOGICAL (AND URBANISTIC) AGENCY OF INFRASTRUCTURE

Chris Reed

Infrastructure by its very nature is anticipatory, even catalytic. While infrastructures typically respond to a set of defined functional needs and requirements, their deployments on the ground, in the city, or across vast territories instantly recontextualize. At their best, they become a new armature for civic or social or economic life; but even as a default, they are a new physical entity to be negotiated, resisted, or appropriated.

Very broadly, twentieth-century infrastructural projects around the world were largely single-minded initiatives, serving very discrete and specialized functional agendas: transportation infrastructures for commerce and exchange, hydrologic infrastructures for power generation and flood control. Toward the end of the century, however, and partly in response to political pressures, infrastructural projects in America and in other countries took on other environmental and sometimes social agendas as well—in the form of mitigation projects that restored a delicate ecological resource or provided a new urban space, for instance. But these mitigation projects were often off-site and unrelated to the primary project at hand. They did not typically affect the core nature of the infrastructure to be built—the essential singularity of such projects remains intact.

Cheonggyecheon is different. At base, the project involves the unearthing of a long- (and twice-) buried natural resource, the Cheonggyecheon River. Yet it is more complex, more rich. It supplants layers of single-minded transportation and flood-control infrastructure with a new kind of hybridized public work: a catalytic agent that spawns new forms of ecological and social life in the city.

Hydrologically, the Cheonggyecheon is multifaceted: part visual amenity, part life-giving resource, part flood-control device. Its sources are largely artificial; though the stream performs an important drainage function for the center of Seoul and its mountain runoff, it lacks consistent volume to sustain its flow. Even pumped water from the city's subways could not maintain what city leaders desired as an adequate regular flow, so they looked elsewhere.

The Cheongge-Ro, 1969.

The culmination of this effort is notable, for both its boldness and its anticipatory stance: pump water from the nearby Han River for now, but set up connections to the city's sewage-treatment plants so that clean effluent from the plants could supply the river in the future, once technology improves. (In fact, the effluent system was tested first, but the visual and olfactory quality of the effluent was not deemed adequate, though technically safe.) So while the current stream flow is a bubbling, gurgling mirage made possible by a not insignificant degree of engineering and effort, the result is a system that can be adapted to new sewage-treatment technologies as they are improved, to new environmental or political agendas over time. City leaders themselves are uncharacteristically open-minded and indeterminate about how the system might change; their approach of "let's see what happens" is refreshing and highly productive—and not so distant an idea from ecologists' models of ecosystems as dynamic, open-ended, and responsive to changing inputs. Governance itself seems to be adapting to more contemporary ideas of how the world works.

In parallel, city leaders almost understate the project's infrastructural agenda, perhaps fearing that the impact of infrastructural requirements on the project might somehow take away from their goals of improved urban lifestyles and a revitalized city. Yet in many ways the requirements of flood control, which were layered in after the project's initial conception and design (the channel was engineered to accommodate a 200-year flood), enrich the project socially and ecologically. By pushing the river and pathways down in elevation (typically 3–5 meters below street level), the project's flood-control agenda spawns a new kind of urban experience—fully enmeshed within the city yet simultaneously apart from it, buffered and quietly engaged, but never entirely removed.

The submerged condition also activates the below-ground city of buried streams, pipes, stormdrains, and outfalls as contributors to the performance and experience

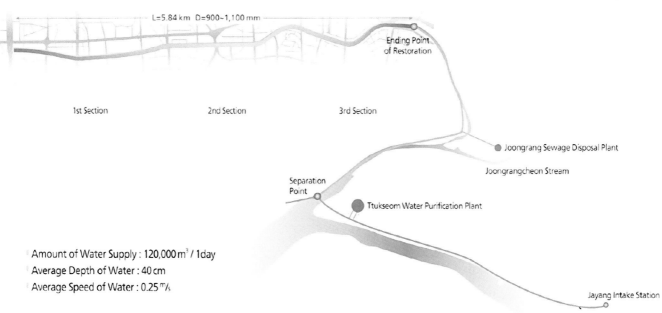

L=5.84 km D=900~1,100 mm

Ending Point
of Restoration

1st Section   2nd Section   3rd Section

Joongrang Sewage Disposal Plant

Joongrangcheon Stream

Separation
Point

Ttukseom Water Purification Plant

Amount of Water Supply : 120,000 m³ / 1day
Average Depth of Water : 40 cm
Average Speed of Water : 0.25 m/s

Jayang Intake Station

Water is pumped from the Han River to the head of the Cheonggyecheon to ensure even flow year-round and optimize the experiential quality of the river.

of the river. Some of these moments are celebrated, like where the Samgak-dong waterscreen and rockfall mark the Cheonggyecheon's intersection with a smaller buried stream and floodway. Historic foundations for buried and outmoded infrastructures, such as the Ogansumum flood-gate, are stabilized and restored. Others, such as modest outfalls, are simply incorporated into riprap slopes; still others are rendered as cutouts of masonry walls, painted to imitate their mineral surrounds. While the latter exam-ple tries to disguise some of the ancillary hydrologic func-tions of the river corridor, none attempt to outright hide it—in some ways, there is no overcoming the channel's essential use of draining a highly urbanized area that gen-erates huge volumes of runoff.

Within the river's floodway, though, a substantial eco-logical agenda is clearly at work: asymmetrical streambanks, high- and low-flow channels, runnels and riffles, eddies and pools are all working to establish a diverse and thriving river ecosystem. Riprap edges work to slow floodwaters and stabilize banks, also creating pockets for small crea-tures to thrive; stepping stones connect pathways on either bank of the river, imitating native river stones; and riffles help to aerate water and establish diverse and healthy habitat. Together, these elements' figuration as part of the linear flood channel is highly artificial in appearance, but functionally and performatively accurate. In fact, it might be argued that the very clearly constructed—even geometricized—versions of indigenous riverine elements speak to an enriched, thickened, and hybridized notion of urban ecology, and of ecological infrastructure.

Most remarkable is the way in which the Cheong-gyecheon spawns and sponsors vibrant new ecological life in the dense city. Massive carp, almost two feet long, swim upstream from the Han River, feeding or taking shelter in the reconstituted river's eddies; they are a stunning discov-ery amid the linear paths and tall walls that separate this magical realm from the bustle of the food markets and hardware shops streetside. In addition, the city's research

Large carp repopulating the Cheonggyecheon from the Han River.

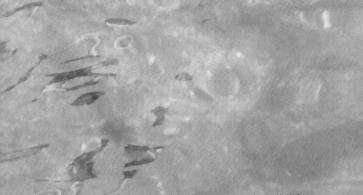

teams have documented a sizable increase in wildlife numbers and diversity since the river's reconstruction: from 4 to 27 fish species (pre-construction and 2009 counts); from 6 to 34 bird species; and from 15 to 206 insect species. Yet the significance is more than statistical: the documented increased diversity at multiple levels of the food chain, and the simple fact that fish such as carp depend on an extended network of healthy interrelationships, speak to the emergent nature of a more complex set of ecological dynamics—a still developing but clearly robust web of new ecologies that are adapting themselves to the conditions at hand. Here is a complex urban ecosystem emerging from the groundwater surcharge of the city's subways and a desire for a clean and pleasant, city-scaled water feature at the center of an economic development initiative. The sheer presence of this emergent ecosystem supplants potential criticism of the artificially flowing river as an example of Disneyfication; in fact, the intertwined agendas of pleasure and leisure, of flood and wastewater control, and of environmental restoration conspire to produce something more rich—and potentially more sustainable—than if the river had been borne of just one agenda alone.

Cheonggyecheon is a deep integration, and rich collusion, of entangled infrastructural, ecological, and social agendas. Given the spatial constraints of its densely packed urban context and the brute functional services it must perform, Cheonggyecheon is a highly sophisticated civic infrastructure in the guise of an urban river restoration. Yet it is not fixed or bounded—it seems to open up as many ecological (and urbanistic) possibilities as it already embodies and supports. Its most potent agency is realized in the numerous ways it spawns and supports new life along its length, and in how these new connections can potentially expand along the broader networks of use and flow, of movement and exchange, and of ecology and culture within which it is now implanted.

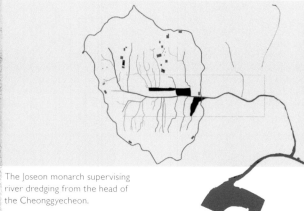

1700 The Geomantic City

The Joseon monarch supervising river dredging from the head of the Cheonggyecheon.

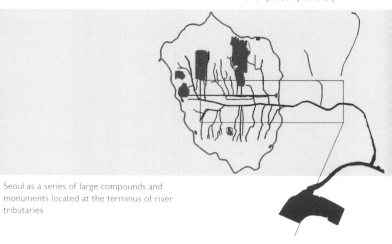

1790 The Temple Compound City

Seoul as a series of large compounds and monuments located at the terminus of river tributaries

1830 The Orthogonal City

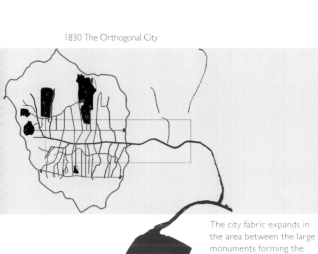

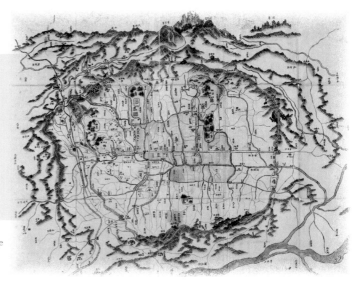

The city fabric expands in
the area between the large
monuments forming the
city center

1903 The Alleyway City

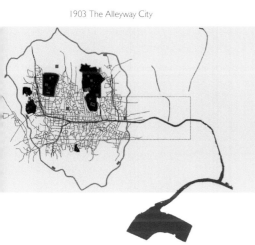

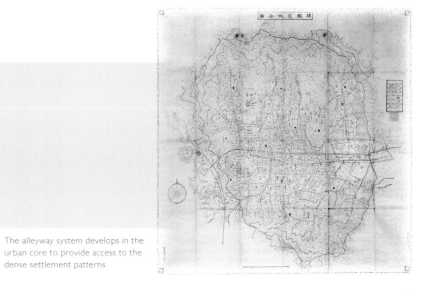

The alleyway system develops in the
urban core to provide access to the
dense settlement patterns

New large-scale urban grid regulates the informal city center, allowing the expansion of the city and the development of new building types.

1937 The Colonial City

The urban core expands along mobility infra-structures—the river and the rail lines—in the space between the mountains.

1958 The Expanded City

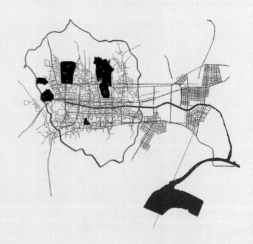

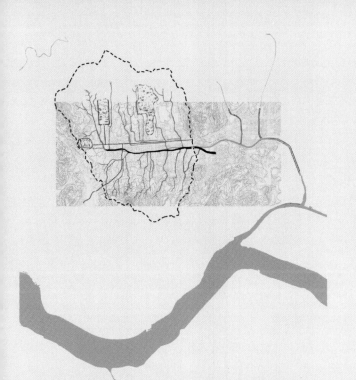

Contemporary urban grid at historical
river and tributary locations.

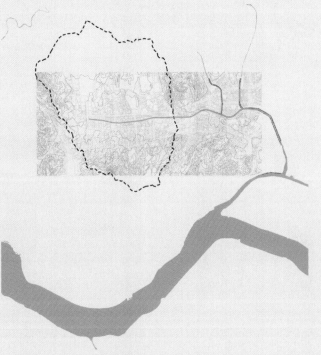

The Cheonggyecheon River and tributaries
forming the central spine of historical Seoul.

REWINDING A PUBLIC INFRASTRUCTURE

Marion Weiss

The economic miracle that transformed Seoul from a city of just over 2 million in 1960 to a city of nearly 11 million today is evident in the density of high-rise structures, highways, and expressways that connect disparate districts. During the rapid urbanization that took place after World War II and the Korean War, Seoul, like many of its western counterparts, built a comprehensive network of roadways and highways to expedite movement within and beyond the idiosyncratic network of streets that formed the core of the old town. Today the core city of Seoul is the center of the second-largest metropolitan area in the world.

The speed of Seoul's urban evolution came at a price. While the surrounding circle of mountains frame a natural perimeter to the city, the devastation of the city's historic fabric during the wars offered an unrestricted territory for unplanned development. The elimination of a dense historic center—and indeed existing natural features such as streams and shallow topographic changes—allowed the city's development to progress without the nuance and character evident in cities with slower urban evolutions.

Lines of Least Resistance

Historically, expedited urban development has led to the construction of highways along the lines of least resistance. Properties without strong individual ownership have presented optimal conditions to superimpose roadways, and politically fragile communities have not had the political strength to protest this signature of progress. Seoul's Cheong-gye Elevated Highway and Cheonggye Road followed such a path, superimposing two layers of roadways over a streambed with a challenged history of flooding and pollution.

This historically natural stream experienced its first infrastructural transformation during the Joseon Dynasty, from 1406 to 1408, when the stream was engineered into a citywide drainage system, part of an overall refurbishment plan. In 1411, bridges were introduced as the stream was dredged and banks were bolstered. At that time, there was no comprehensive drainage system, and the stream eventually became a central open drainage path for people living in Seoul. The shallowness of the water led to

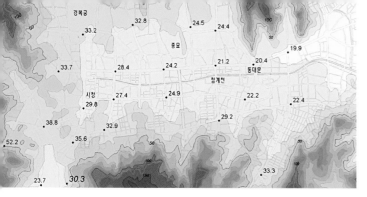

pollution and disease, and the constant dredging needed to remove the river basin's sediment and sludge required a feat of engineering by teams of horses and men.

By the middle of the twentieth century, the territory along the stream evolved as an economically and politically marginalized part of the city—paradoxically located along the geographically central spine of Seoul. The economic and ecological vulnerability of this territory created an almost inevitable opening for the creation of the Cheonggye Elevated Highway. Built between 1967 and 1971, the elevated highway covered this streambed, simultaneously creating unencumbered passage through the central business district of the city and ensuring the continued marginal status of the urban community along its nearly 3-mile-length.

Infrastructural Exhaustion / A New Beginning

On the surface, the covering of the Cheonggyecheon stream appeared to be a case study of urban improvement. Any negative impact of a monofunctional infrastructure on this challenged area was peripheral to Seoul's commitment to a mobile, autocentric future. Throughout the developed world, the postwar creation of expressways and highways became the signature of urban development and density. Ironically, in Seoul, the same concern for public health that legitimized the removal of a stream to create a highway more than thirty years ago resurfaced as a motivator to remove the highway and restore the stream.

Indeed, Mayor Myung-bak Lee chose the removal of the highway and the restoration of Cheonggyecheon as the central platform for his campaign in 2002. His commitment to improving the quality of life indices and restoring health to the city focused on the imperative of removing the highway and restoring the stream. While the transformation of stream to highway evolved from 1958 to 1977 within the objective criteria of transportation design, Mayor Lee had the more complex obligation to establish and disseminate new terms and metrics defining an infinitely more subjective subject: quality of urban life.

Many political leaders have staked their legacies on urban transformations, but Mayor Lee set an unprecedented benchmark for speed and effectiveness, developing the proposal within months of his election and completing the project twenty-seven months after the beginning of the design process. With a diverse team of leaders from universities, government, businesses, and ad hoc public

left The city grew rapidly to fill the area between the hills and the mountains.
below Prior to covering, the streambed was neglected and polluted.

groups, he effectively articulated the economic and cultural imperative to destroy the highway and restore the stream.

The city approached the creation of this project with a comprehensive agenda, conceived with the motivation of a pending political election and deployed with the strategic clarity of a military operation. Both process and implementation were conducted publically, but unlike the more glacially paced implementation processes familiar in North America, the demolition of the highway and stream restoration were realized with Seoul's signature effectiveness and speed. The success and unprecedented speed of this infrastructural transformation reflects a comprehensive vision combined with deft political navigation.

Infrastructure, Artifice, and Ecology

The burial of the stream that signaled a commitment to progress during the postwar years has now been paradoxically replaced with a new signature of progress, a nearly 3-mile infrastructure of slowness, an urban theater with ecological and cultural ambitions. Crossed by twenty-seven bridges, the stream/park begins at the city level within a public plaza, descends below the city level to create a sub-city promenade through Seoul's central business district, and terminates in a natural ecological corridor that connects to a 280-acre forest preserve. A hybrid of urban destination and transformative engineering, the renovated stream is an infrastructural chameleon—equally programmed as civic space, urban retreat, historic interpretive

center, sequential water garden, and ecological restoration. The project creates a new reciprocity between engineered nature and a vibrant public life.

An Unprecedented Urban Section

There are few examples of successful public realms that reside below the level of the city. In fact, the urge to create a double-thickness urban fabric has been part of Modernist and pre-Modernist utopian visions. Hugh Ferris, in his "Metropolis" series, rendered a multileveled city of inhabitable bridges and connecting public concourses twelve stories above the level of the city. Corbusier, in his unrealized designs for Algiers and Rio de Janeiro, identified a new hybrid of highway and continuous housing, and in the decades following World War II, the Metabolists, largely centered in Japan, rendered a vision of multilevel cities that might sustain the anticipated explosive growth of urban centers around the world. These utopian visions all anticipated a density that would support the demands of multilevel urban public realm; in all of these examples, subcity-level public identities were never imagined.

Elevated linear urban additions to cities along the site of former infrastructural corridors have seen recent success in Paris with Promenade Plantée, designed in 1987 and completed in 2000 by Jacques Vergely (landscape architect) and Philippe Mathieux (architect); in Seattle with Weiss/Manfredi's Olympic Sculpture Park (2008); and in New York City with Field Operations and Diller Scofidio + Renfro's High Line (2010). Promenade Plantée, the precursor to the High Line, creates an elevated park on the top of a viaduct while inhabiting its continuous arcade with shops. The Olympic Sculpture Park establishes a new continuous landform that crosses highways and train lines to connect the city and waterfront with a new sculpture park; the High Line appropriates a slender elevated train line to create a continuous linear garden raised above the city. San Antonio's River Walk counts on its immediate association with the level of the city it travels through to create the vibrant, if nostalgic, district. Each of these examples creates a public territory coincident with or above the city level.

Twenty-four Feet Below: A Retreat from the City

Offering a new addition to successful urban redistributions or reappropriations of infrastructure, the Cheonggyecheon restoration offers a fundamentally different paradigm. By contrast, this project offers a more architectural, more intimate relationship with water—more akin to a promenade through a skylit museum gallery animated by the movement and sound of water.

The project is a sectional chameleon, a kind of parallel city. While it begins at the city level with an urban plaza designed for large-scale urban events, it descends below the cross-traffic level, providing unbroken passage through the city while simultaneously accommodating necessary flood control. The steep drop of the section produces a kind of contemporary reverse fortification, with bilevel landscapes and walks that induce a slower pace. In some moments, the steep concrete walls that define the core of the linear park produce the sensation of being displaced in a linear gallery of water and promenades, distinct and independent from the city that hovers 24 feet above. At the terminus of the constructed precinct of the city, these concrete walls recline back into a natural edge, broadening the width of the park and bringing an ecological corridor under a network of

existing elevated on-ramps and off-ramps. Most important, the Cheonggyecheon restoration project is extraordinarily successful as a public infrastructure, a retreat, an ecological contribution to the city, and the a new public level.

This project invents a slender water course centered within a subsurface retreat from the city—cool, tranquil, with a soundscape of water concealing the noise of traffic above. The project's identity oscillates between a massive infrastructural undertaking and a finely detailed garden of delights.

A New Paradigm

The project asks a profound question: Can we deploy the Cheonggyecheon River as a different kind of paradigm or a collection of paradigms, against the failings of monofunctionalist urbanism? The project translates a dream, a microcosm of all that was lost, into a fully engineered urban infrastructure for public life, generating a radiating set of urban improvements along its rejuvenated spine. The project, a massive infrastructure undertaking, simultaneously engineers a new stormwater management transformation and constructs the artifice of nature at the heart of the city.

As a public infrastructure, the project defines a new cultural expression, integral to a city's experience and growth, not marginalized as a bit of necessary embellishment after the planners, finance committees, and political performers have made all of their decisions. The project demonstrates that large-scale initiatives do not have to be destructive: the cultures of architecture, landscape architecture, engineering, design, planning, commercial development, and community activism can find common purpose. The sheer optimism and audacity of the project, its speedy realization and profound contribution to public life, confirms Seoul's commitment to engineering a renewed relationship between infrastructure, nature, and public life.

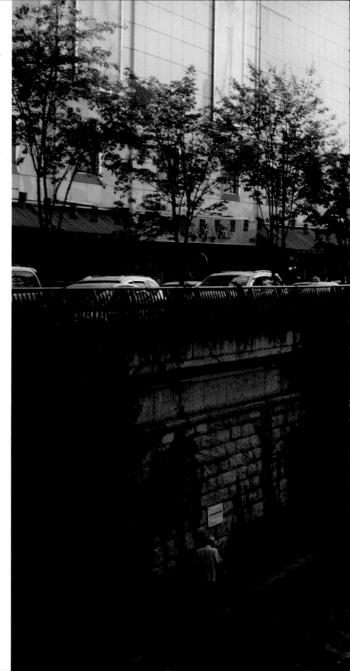

In Seoul, we see an intermeshing between an ideal "maxi-grid" system—perfectly orthogonal and evenly metered—and the influence of the city's considerable topography to create a hybrid grid system that retains the recognizable characteristics of the grid while embracing its distinctive physical context. The city's foundational maxi-grid straddled the Cheonggyecheon, with the river itself playing one of its component members. Over time, the same logic is used in the development of other city subsectors to create a multinodal yet related city across a broad territory.

During the first half of the nineteenth century, significant efforts were made to rationalize the alleyway urbanism along the river through a Haussmann-like approach of cutting the existing fabric to create a rectilinear maxi-grid and Beaux-Arts style connecting diagonals. This approach led to broader, straighter street layouts to increase capacity, necessitating extreme demolition work.

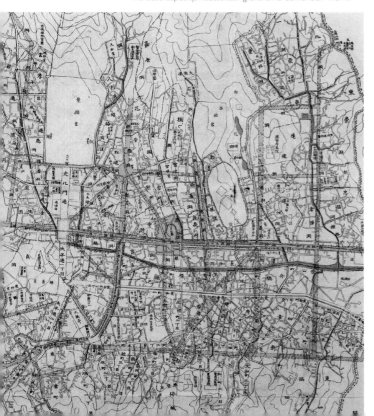

The early maxi-grid was formed around the Cheonggyecheon, with the river as the central east-west axis. This grid created a series of large blocks, each cut by small alleyways to provide access to the interior.

The maxi-grid of the city expanded along the river. Outside the boundaries of the historical wall, the grid was implimented tabula rasa, with a regular mini-scale grid within.

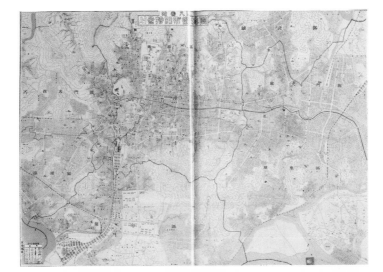

Large boulevards cut the dense fabric.

Development of the grid over time along the river.

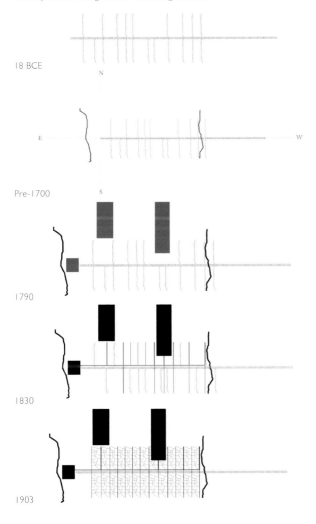

18 BCE

N

E — W

S

Pre-1700

1790

1830

1903

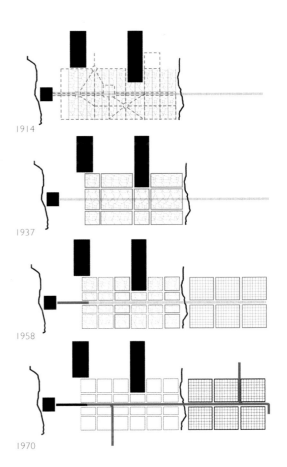

1914

1937

1958

1970

MEASURING TRANSFORMATION: EFFECTS OF THE RESTORATION WORK

Heung-Sun Kim, Tae-Gyu Koh, and Kie-Wook Kwon
(text excerpted and edited by Ian Klein)

The Cheonggyecheon Restoration Project was launched with a public ceremony on July 1, 2003. More than 2,000 people gathered at the entrance to the elevated highway passing over the stream, which would be removed in three parts: Sector 1, Taepyeongro to Gwangjang Market (2km); Sector 2, Gwangjang Market to Nangyero (2.1km); and Sector 3, Nangyero to Sindap Railroad Bridge (1.7km). Work began with the removal of the ten concrete ramp sections, followed by the removal of the 5,817-meter-long upper plates and 371 piers of the elevated highway. Following this, the concrete covering the stream, the 6,700 piers supporting the concrete structures, and the seven pedestrian overpasses were removed. This work was carried out until the end of August 2003; the job of removing the concrete structures covering the stream was conducted between August 13, 2003, and the end of May 2004. Removal of the elevated highway linking Cheonggye 1-ga with Namsan No. 1 Tunnel was done between mid-August and October 5, 2003. The new Cheonggyecheon opened to the public on October 1, 2005. The number of visitors exceeded 10 million in just 58 days, 50 million in 617 days, and 75.5 million by the end of 2008, or an average of 64,000 a day. The urban effects of this massive project can be measured in a number of ways.

Social and Cultural Effects

According to a survey undertaken by the Seoul Development Institute in 2005 of 1,000 Seoulites who visited Cheonggyecheon, 54.7 percent said that the restored stream was an appealing place to visit. The site has also drawn many people from outside of Seoul, emerging as a leading tourist attraction. Among the 75.5 million people who visited the restored stream by the end of 2008, 24 percent were non-Seoulites.

The Cheonggyecheon Restoration Project enhanced the symbolic importance of Seoul as the country's historical and cultural center. The work made it possible to excavate and restore artifacts of cultural heritage that had remained unseen for decades due to the concrete structure covering the stream. At facilities placed along the Cheonggyecheon, cultural events—folk events, concerts, exhibitions, poetry readings—are held almost every day, making the stream a center for public activities in Seoul.

Economic Impact

It is expected that the restored stream will help Gangbuk (the area in Seoul north of the Han River) regain its competitiveness against Gangnam (the southern area). The dilapidated urban structure of the area acted as a powerful damper to Seoul's competitiveness compared to that of other cities in Northeast Asia. Over the past decade, the population in Gangbuk has decreased by 80,000. Urban refurbishment projects in Gangbuk had failed to attract private capital. Following the completion of the restoration work, a large number of upscale multipurpose buildings are being built along the Cheonggyecheon, causing the price of real estate to rise at a rate higher than that in Gangnam. According to the Seoul Development Institute, the price of land in the area close to Seun Arcade jumped by 50 percent, from 40 million won to 60 million won. Even in Inhyeon-dong, a block from the Cheonggyecheon, the price of land appears to have risen by 30 percent in the same period. This is double the rate of increase in other areas in Seoul.

Environmental Improvements

The restoration of the stream as a clean and natural body of water running through the heart of the city became an irrefutable signal of the transformation of Seoul into an ecologically friendly metropolis. It appears that after the restoration work, the number of wildlife species increased from 98 to 626. Between the pre-restoration work period and the end of 2008, the number of plant species found in the area increased from 62 to 308, fish species from 4 to 27, bird species from 6 to 34, aquatic invertebrate species from 5 to 53, insect species from 15 to 206, mammals from 2 to 4, and amphibians from 4 to 8. Indigenous fish species, such as Korean minnows (*Zacco koreanus*) and Korean spined loaches (*Iksookimia koreensis*) were newly found after the restoration work. Many other species posted an increase through spawning, demonstrated an improved suitability for life within the natural ecological system. In the lower stream areas, grasshoppers (*Locusta migratoria*), a species specially protected by the City of Seoul, were spotted for three straight years, indicating that the streamside grassland is developing into a desirable terrestrial insect habitat.

As for bird species, common kestrels, highly valued in Korea and thus protected, were found, along with great titmice (*Parus major*), river kingfishers (*Alcedo atthis*), and swallows, also protected. Korean salamanders (also *protected*), lizards (*Takydromus wolteri*), and frogs were found. About 308 kinds of plants were discovered, including calico flower (*Aristolochia littoralis*), *Stellaria media Cvrillus*, Oriental false hawksbeards (*Youngia japonica*), honeyweeds (*Leonurus sibiricus*), *Fallopia dumetora*, Polygonaceae (*Persicaria hydropiper*), and variable leaf yellowcress (*Rorippa indica*).

Climate Melioration

The restored stream acts as a cooling agent against the urban heat-island effect. The Seoul Development Institute's analysis of temperature changes after the completion of the restoration work showed a 10 percent lowering of the maximum temperature. Thermal imaging also estimated a 2 to 5 percent lowering of the temperature at various points. It is expected that the effect of the restoration work will turn out to be greater when other factors are taken into account: its cooling effect on the artificial heat transfer of vehicle engines running in the area, the heat accumulation and transfer of the asphalt pavement, and the energy diffusion from buildings in the area. Additionally, the creation of streamside wind corridors due to the restoration work, through which masses of cool air can move, mitigates the urban heat-island effect. Analysis shows a higher wind speed (i.e., by an average of 2.2 to 7.1 percent) both on the street and at streamside areas.

Circulation Effects

According to an analysis of the traffic situation between June 2003 and December 2005, it appears that the restored stream has had little impact on the flow of traffic in the area, which typically accommodates speeds of 17 to 18 kilometers per hour during the morning rush hour and 12 kilometers per hour during the evening rush hour. The number of people using buses (based on those using traffic cards) increased by 15.1 percent, following a reorganization of the public transportation system. The number of people using the subway increased by 3.3 percent throughout Seoul and by 9 percent downtown, compared to June 2003. It is judged that more people now choose to use public transportation since the removal of the elevated highway over the Cheonggyecheon, and thus the restored stream does not have a negative impact on the overall traffic situation. The number of people using subway trains serving routes between Gangnam/Gangseo and downtown decreased a little, whereas the number of subway users on routes between the northeastern section and downtown increased. It is speculated that many of the people who formerly used the elevated highway and the Cheonggyecheon-ro switched to use of the subway after the stream restoration work began.

—Adapted from a presentation prepared for the International Conference on World Class Sustainable Cities 2009, Rennaissance Hotel, Kuala Lumpur, Malaysia, March 24, 2009.

ILLUSTRATION CREDITS

Veronica Rudge Green Prize in Urban Design

2007
Olympic Sculpture Park for the Seattle Art Museum
Weiss/Manfredi: Architecture, Landscape, Urbanism

2005
Aleppo: Rehabilitation of the Old City
City of Aleppo

2002
Residential Waterfront: Borneo Sporenburg, Amsterdam
Adriaan Geuze, West 8 Urban Design and Landscape Architecture

2000
The Favela-Bairro Project, Rio de Janeiro
Jorge Mario Jáuregui Architects

1998
The Carré d'Art, Nîmes, and the Bilbao Metro
Foster and Partners

1996
Restoration of the Historic Center of Mexico City, and the Ecological Restoration of the District of Xochimilco
Mexico City

1993
Hillside Terrace Complex, Tokyo
Fumihiko Maki

and

The Master Plan and Public Buildings of Monte Carasso, Switerland
Luigi Snozzi

1990
The Urban Public Spaces of Barcelona
City of Barcelona

1988
Byker Redevelopment in Newcastle Upon Tyne
Ralph Erskine

and

Malagueira Quarter Housing Project in Evora, Portugal
Alvaro Siza Viera